"The single most powerful asset we have is our mind, if trained well, it can create enormous wealth."

- Robert Kiyosaki

ADVENTAGO

This book is dedicated to all the entrepreneurs whom I have been called to serve, all of you have made it possible for me to do the work that interests me, and that I feel is meaningful to the world.

This book was created to help you stand strong and tall, no matter what the world tries to throw at you, so you can serve and uplift the people, that are waiting to hear your message.

If this book helps you reach just one more person, and change their life with your God-given gifts, then this work will have been a success.

Table of Contents

The Fastest Way On How To Make Your Business Sustainable And Profitable Part 1

I was 35 years old, I had 9,094 stores around the world, everyone loved me, I had a worldwide market value of $5 billion, I thought that I would live forever...

Can you guess who I am? You've probably been there yourself more than once, it's no other than BlockBuster.

You probably remember renting your movies or video games and desperately trying to binge-watch everything before you sadly had to give it back, but why do I use this as an example?

It's not to scare you but to present to you what is possible in the cutthroat world of business, if one of the biggest giants in business can fall to its knees then no one can hide.

The great thing is you aren't burying your head in the sand or letting your ego get the best of you.

For you to be reading this book you are trying to educate yourself on ways to improve the sustainability and profits of your organization.

Let's get started with the first effective way to build a sustainable and profitable business.

Don't Be Desperate

Starting a business when you are desperate is a bad idea, the reason why is that you are going to make extremely emotional decisions.

That may not be beneficial for the company, there seems to be a trend in people thinking, "If I'm broke, I'll just start my own business"

What they don't understand is that you're the king of the business, but you eat last at the table, since you are giving money to others to keep your business alive.

Also, you might not even see any money coming in for a long time, since business is a risky process and won't drop money into your lap the next day.

You Have A Clear Business Model

Now you have a business idea, the next step is how are you going to monetize it? And how is it going to stand out from your competition?

This is when you get into the nitty gritty details of where you see your company, and how it's going to get attention.

For example, are you going to sell a product for $100, then have an upsell for $1,000 then lastly have a members only area for $10,000?

This is a simple example but, the point is you need a model and a pathway that you are going to guide your customers through.

The reason why is that you don't want to have a onetime customer but a raving fan that is over the moon to buy from you again.

You Have A Clear Money-Making Path

This means you have a clear idea of how you are going to make sales and get customers through the door, it doesn't have to be a stampede of people.

But, you should have a clear idea of the techniques you are going to use to get someone to buy from you.

Unfortunately, this is the problem with many startup businesses, they have an amazing product.

But don't know how to sell it, so they hope that if they build the best product that customers will magically find them.

This is not a sensible strategy to have, so before you launch, know who your ideal customers are and make sure you can speak to them.

Another thing you must keep an eye on is that the sale is profitable.

This is especially important since a lot of entrepreneurs get extremely excited that they made their first sale.

However, if it cost $4 to get your customer and your product is only $1 then you have made a negative return.

You need to have methods in your head that will allow you to get customers without costing you an arm and a leg.

You Have An Advantage

This can be some type of unfair advantage that makes your head stick out of the noisy marketplace.

If you don't give your customers a good reason to come to you or switch from what they currently have, then you're just going to be another fish in a big ocean.

By the way, I need to let you know that simply saying "My product is better" is not a strong enough reason.

A better example would be, you have better advertising, you have connections to influencers, or, you know the industry from a consumer's perspective.

Anything that you can think of that will give you the leg up in your career as an entrepreneur.

You Have Capital

This means you have money to get started and to keep on going, a lot of entrepreneurs only save up enough money to get the ball.

But few think about how much it will cost to keep it rolling, and, almost no one thinks about having a cushion in case things go wrong.

Also, if you don't have enough capital, you're going to have to make decisions based on price, which can be a pain if you know there are better options, but you can't afford them.

Make sure to have enough money set aside to be able to handle anything that may come up.

How Much Capital Do I Need?

This depends on business to business, but a good rule of thumb is to have 6 months of savings, and have access to other methods of cash.

This could be a bank, friend, or private lender, this enables you to make better decisions and keep your business afloat in case issues arise.

50% of businesses fail within the first 2 years, 90 to 95% fail within the first 5 years, we've all heard this statistic before, but these numbers need to burn into your head.

That your chance of survival is very low, and even if you do beat these statistics, how long are you're going to last?

I know you're going to say "But Adventago I'm the exception!"

Everyone thinks the same way, no one believes they're going to be in the bucket of ones who fail, therefore you can sometimes be a bit too optimistic with your business idea.

I'm not saying you can't make it, but I'm here to warn you that you should look at your business as an investor, by asking yourself these questions, what could go wrong? And how can I prevent it?

I believe this is due to how the media has perceived being an entrepreneur, that you're this cool boss that has a billion-dollar company.

With bottles, models, mansions, Lamborghinis, and fat paychecks, but the reality is there are a lot of entrepreneurs who die.

I hope this chapter gave you some insight on what to do next, however, I understand you may want proven steps to your success.

If you're frustrated that you haven't made your first sale or you want a constant stream of customers, then type this link into your browser.

↓

bit.ly/bonusbook9

To go straight to a video called, the profit boot camp.

This is where you can discover methods to increase your business's recognition, and, help you get from dreaming of being an entrepreneur, to becoming an entrepreneur.

What would you do if you had more abundance, wealth, and success in your life? And how many lives would you positively impact?

Type this link into your browser to get instant access to your answer to getting past the hurdle of your first sale now!

↓

<u>bit.ly/bonusbook9</u>

The Fastest Way On How To Make Your Business Sustainable And Profitable Part 2

Welcome back! I see that you are eager to discover more about how to make your business sustainable and profitable.

This chapter will go into what I call the business pyramid, it's a list of all the things a business needs to be bulletproof in difficult situations.

I have a disclaimer before we continue: The list goes from the most important up to the least important.

However, this doesn't mean that you can slack off, and not work on all the factors, or else your business will fail.

Without any more delay, let's get started, this is what the business pyramid looks like.

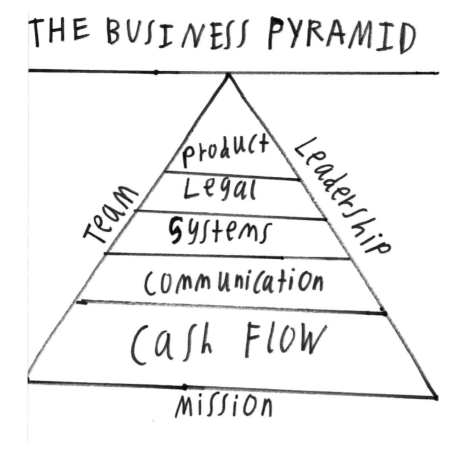

THE BUSINESS PYRAMID

Product
Leadership
Team
Legal
Systems
Communication
Cash Flow
Mission

Mission

This is your why in your business, why did you start a business in the first place? What drives you to build this empire?

You need to be able to share this passion with others, so they can see your vision in your business too.

If you have a strong mission, and a clear path as to why you are constantly working hard, then you won't feel discouraged when things go wrong.

However, if the drive for your business is weak, or, no longer relevant you will slowly start to see a decline in your work ethic and interest.

This comes back to the issue of starting a business just to make money, which is what a lot of entrepreneurs tend to do, but this isn't a spiritual reason.

That type of reason will quickly die when you hit obstacles, a better mission is needing the money to take care of your sick mother.

You can see this example in charities, why would you want to work there if it's volunteer, or, low pay? The reason why is due to their spiritual calling, that they want to help the world and leave a legacy.

I'm not saying you have to make a charity, but, try and boil down the reason that will make you and others feel uplifted when times get rough.

Many businesses are selling the same products, and the customers are starting to feel colder in making decisions.

However, if they see that you're working towards something more than just a transaction, then they will almost feel obligated to give you their attention and cash.

This is why companies have slogans, because, it's a message that they want to bake into the customer's mind, NO! We aren't just PlayStation.

"We are for the players", this makes people feel reassured that this company isn't just after boosting their revenue, but, is here to deliver a great service.

"But I Don't Know My Mission."

There is a bit of a downfall to the mission being the most important thing, since a lot of entrepreneurs think too deeply about their mission.

To the point they aren't taking action, and, getting their business started, but Adventago "I just want to make more money".

I understand on the outside this could be true, but just like the example, I said before, why do you want money? Surely, it's not just because you like colorful paper.

Remember this mission doesn't have to be about the product, you could be selling flowers and your mission is that you want to provide for your kids, however, if you are stuck, I have a few suggestions.

- You have so much valuable information that you want to share it with others.
- You want to help others.
- You want to pass it on to someone you love and trust.
- You want to build a legacy.
- You want a business so you can keep busy.
- You want to put your skills to good work, and teach them valuable life skills.

All these reasons can get you thinking since your mission should be unique to you.

For example, I made the blog Adventago.com because I would learn from many mentors, but the problem is.

I would never document it, so after a day, I would forget everything I learned.

This led to me writing things down, which was a good idea, until I had so much information that the papers were getting too big.

So, I thought instead of writing all of this in word documents, I could share this with others on the internet, and, that's how Adventago.com was born, as you can see my mission isn't anything fancy but it's a valid one.

Give it some thought, I'm sure you have something amazing in that entrepreneurial mind of yours.

Team

Business is not golf, you aren't playing one on one, it's a team rowing race, everyone needs to do their part, or, else you will be defeated by others.

This is the problem with the school system, it teaches you to shut up and work alone, and, if you talked to someone, or, used the internet it's classed as "Cheating".

But, we all know in life, every job application asks you to be…

A Team Player!

This is why you need to get rid of the brainwashing that being with others is cheating.

It doesn't matter how smart you are, it's a huge stress to do everything yourself, so, why not leverage other people's expertise so you can focus on what you're best at?

You won't believe how many business owners do their taxes just because they want to avoid paying a tax advisor.

I say to them "Why on earth would you do them yourself, you aren't an accountant, also you could be missing out on opportunities to reduce tax".

But How Can I Afford A Team?

This question usually comes from people who don't understand taxes, and, aren't making a lot of money in their business.

What happens is that business owners pay their expenses first before they pay taxes.

This means they have more money before taxes to pay their team, and, even less net income leftover for the government to tax.

It also comes from people who say "But business is risky" this mostly comes from the thought of being a one-man show, and, trying to juggle everything on your own.

What they don't understand is that they can have others who are masters in their field and can educate you.

Another thing I see is the confusion of a team and a gathering, take for example a teacher's union, this is a group of teachers who all do the same thing.

However, the team I'm talking about is people who come together with completely different skills, just like Fast And Furious.

Is The Team Of A Certain Level?

This is something investors look for before putting their money into a business, does the business have a high-level team? This means is everyone at the optimal level in their field.

If an investor sees that you have a great accountant, but, an awful sales team, then the investors know it's going to be difficult for you to get, more customers.

Also, you want to position yourself as the "Go to company" For example, if you were offered a job that you wanted at Apple would you take it up?

Probably yes, because you know that Apple will take good care of you, and, they have a good track record for being successful.

You can use this to your advantage to acquire people who are very skilled even if you can't afford them.

If people can see that you are a competent business owner they will stick around, because, they know you will make it big eventually.

Your Mentor

If you can learn from someone who has skill in making a great team then you can become one too, this is why the most successful people learned from someone successful.

Why go through all the trouble trying to make a good team when you can learn from someone who has already built one?

Leadership

Every team needs a leader, their role is to gather a team, have them work successfully, bring out the best in people, and, be a role model to look up to.

This is why most people don't like to be the leader since working with people can be a huge headache at times.

I want to let you know before you say "But Adventago I'm not a leader", you have to understand that no one was born a leader, a true leader is made, and, is willing to be trained by others.

As a leader, you must be able to motivate your people, this makes everyone feel empowered and want to stay with you even in the hard times, it also makes people want to work harder.

You need to be a visionary, so you can see the future of your company and make up new strategies that will evolve you.

This is why Dan Lok closes his door, and unplugs his phone, so he can think of new ideas, he calls it his "Bat cave moment".

Another thing a leader needs is brutal execution, I know it can be sad and scary, but, there are going to be times you have to put your foot down.

For example, telling someone they are working poorly, or worse having to watch an employee cry because you have to fire them.

These scenarios shouldn't happen all the time, but the day-to-day of making decisions should be inside of you, or else you will miss out on opportunities.

Without leadership, there is nothing but chaos, you need to be able to put everyone in check and point your crew to victory.

These three sides are very important to a business, if you don't have these in proper shape, then you aren't going to last as an entrepreneur.

Type this link into your browser to get instant access to your answer to becoming an unstoppable business owner.

↓

bit.ly/bonusbook9

The Fastest Way On How To Make Your Business Sustainable And Profitable Part 3

YAY! We are here with part 3, of what makes a sustainable and profitable business, this is going to cover the insides of the pyramid and how they can save your business in any situation.

As a refresher here is what the business pyramid looks like.

THE BUSINESS PYRAMID

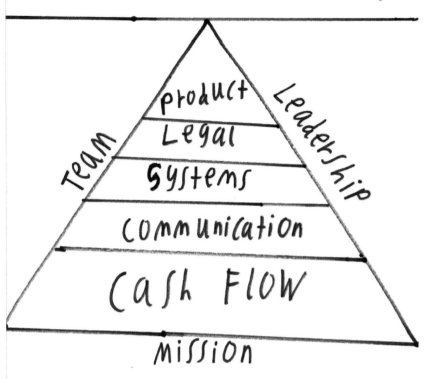

Cash Flow

This is a seriously important factor for any business to stay successful, it's why you should learn how to read a financial statement so you can analyze the numbers and truth behind a company.

This is why Warren Buffet looks at the business's cash flow first, and, guesses the price of the company based on his analysis, instead of letting the price dictate his thoughts.

If you were to ask the most financially literate people like accountants, bankers, and loan officers they will say to you that a vast majority of people are weak, or, clueless about financial literacy.

I had a friend who asked me "What the hell is an interest rate?" at first, I wanted to scold him and the education system for not making people aware of these terms, but, I bit my tongue and explained to him.

It's very sad to see so many people who are completely clueless about these simple tips, tricks, and techniques, that would swing major doors in their financial future.

This is also a problem in companies, the CEO may be very smart and profitable, but, may not know the difference between cash flow and profit, which eventually leads to the business becoming broke.

Drum this into your head, the importance of cash flow, since it's the difference between a small business and a big business.

If you are still a bit confused as to why cash flow is important, think of it as the blood to a human body, it's great that you have blood, but, it doesn't mean anything if it can't be circulated.

This is the same for a business, if you don't get this sorted out then it's going to haunt you.

This is why you see major companies have a steady stream of income in some sort of subscription, the reason they do this instead of letting you pay one time, is so they can get a constant flow of cash, which is a huge lifesaver for any company.

Since it means if anything comes up, they can pay off their expenses that are due, take Netflix for example, they own most of the bandwidth on the planet since people are streaming movies in high quality.

If Netflix were to let you view as many movies as you desire for a one-time purchase, they would be broke very quickly, since they have to keep up with their recurring costs.

Also, they would have to acquire a new customer every time, which would freak them out when they don't meet the number of sales needed.

Or, they would have to charge you a ridiculous one-time payment, so, they can remain profitable.

This is something you are looking for too in your journey as an entrepreneur, but you call it passive income.

Think of cash flow as passive income for a business, it lets the business sit back and relax, while it does the hard work up front, then gets paid every time.

This is why not having one single type of subscription plan is a dangerous decision for your business, just ask Tesla It's no fun trying to sell a car every day.

Do You Have Any Tips?

Don't worry, I won't just tell you what's wrong without some tips you can use to take action, here are some simple ways you can have great cash flow.

- Delay taking a salary until your business is generating cash flow from your sales, in some cases this may not be possible due to an extended development period, however, your investors will be much more appreciated if they see that you are sharing in the development process by investing your time.

- Keep your job and have your business as a side hustle, this stops you from having to dig into your business to take care of yourself, you can quit your job when your business can cover your living expenses.

- Quickly send payments to your customers when you do a service, this stops the awkward delay that a customer doesn't pay you which could lead to headaches of you chasing people for money.

- Charge first then do your service, this is the fastest way to make sure you have cash flow, since you know you will never miss a day, of your money since it's coming straight to you.

- Accept electronic payments we aren't in the stone ages anymore, you won't believe how many small businesses only accept cash, I know there are reasons why, but if you want to expand your business and become something bigger than just a corner shop you have to get with the times.

- Ask to extend or reduce costs, you won't believe how many people shake when I tell them you can negotiate with your credit card company to reduce the interest, or, extend the payment time, this is the same thing you can do in your business if you are a good customer and have a decent track record of being on time with your payments you can negotiate on terms.

- Keep your overhead to a minimum, a good rule of thumb is to increase your sales before you buy a new product, this prevents the worry of, "If this doesn't work then…" , It's also why a lot of people have online businesses, since they know it's the future, and, there's less stress, so next time you have a task maybe think about how you can automate it, or, use special software.
- Have an investment plan when you have money left over that can be put to better use.
- Establish a relationship with one bank.
- Establish a good and solid team to handle the finances and number crunching (Or find a good and solid software).
- Make it easy to get paid, no one wants to jump through hurdles just to give you money, this is why you should be as straightforward and diversified in how you can be paid, (Would you really want your competitors stealing your customers just because you don't accept card?).
- Have enough cash around to handle chargebacks, banks mostly side with the customers, and this can mean if there's a dispute about money, the bank can just go into your account and take out the money, and,

give it to the customer, as an entrepreneur you want to be cautious of this.

These may sound easy or complicated to you but if you do want further detail, I recommend you get an accountant that can help you with all your money management, however, this doesn't mean you can switch off.

As the final shot caller, you should still understand the numbers and get into the habit of looking at your financial statements every day, so, you can strategize for the days to come.

Communication

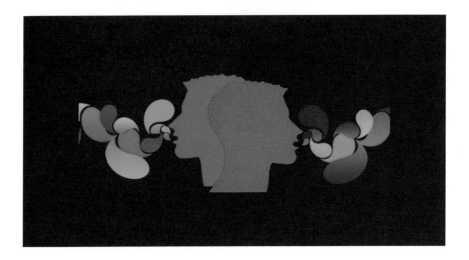

The better you are at communicating the better you will be in life, you need to be able to get your point across in a sensible, compelling, and understanding way.

This is why most successful companies have a CEO that is great at closing prospects, the way to get good at this is by understanding human psychology.

Unfortunately, you won't get many sales just because you're passionate about your product, and you hope the more you talk about it, the more the other person is going to have the same passion.

This is visible in a lot of entrepreneurs, they believe since they love their idea their enthusiasm will rub off on others, you see a lot of this on Shark Tank, and, Dragons Den.

But you have to know, what makes the other person tick, and how you can use that to your advantage.

The art of sales is extremely difficult since it's never a one size fits all, everyone has different buttons that need pushing to make a successful deal.

You could probably tell me a person that has an amazing talent, or, invention that would change the world, but you wonder to yourself "Why hasn't this person been recognized yet?"

The reason is due to lack of communication, you have to be able to get your voice heard in the noisy marketplace, this is a skill that needs to be learned, or else you will be forgotten, as the saying goes.

"Many People Are Talking But Only A Few Are Listening"

I'm surprised to see how little business owners work on their communication skills, since cash flowing into your business is communication flowing out.

You tend to find that businesses struggle because of poor or lack of communication, this doesn't mean just being a good salesperson.

You also have to monitor the communication happening internally, for example, are your employees cooperating or trying to do things their own way?

You probably think that this is something you will focus on later, but if you don't get your communication skills up to level.

You may not be able to raise capital to get your business started, this is an extremely difficult situation to be in since raising capital is an entrepreneur's most important job.

This doesn't mean that the entrepreneur is constantly begging for money, but what it means is that the entrepreneur has the reassurance to get more capital if needed.

This is very important in the early stages of your business since you need to have a constant stream of cash to keep your business growing.

If you are one of those people who hate selling then I wish you luck, since it's not going to end well for you, also if you are one of those people who are scared to sell.

Then don't worry there are plenty of events and teachings you can go to learn on how to be better at selling.

For example, a live event Dan Lok used to go to when he was young was called Toastmaster.

According to Wikipedia - Toastmasters International is a US-headquartered nonprofit educational organization that operates clubs worldwide for the purpose of promoting communication, public speaking, and leadership.

Are Marketing And Sales The Same Thing?

I had to get my head around the difference between sales and marketing too, I would eventually learn that these are two very important factors that makeup communication.

If a business has good sales this means it can close the deal on prospects, on the other hand.

If a business has good marketing, it means they have made an efficient system that can get customers interested in them.

As you can see marketing is to get people through the door, and sales is to seal the deal and get your prospect to buy.

Many sales professionals will say that once you learn to sell you need to learn how to market.

This is the difference between a small business and a large business.

Small businesses may be good at getting you to buy if you visit their store, but a big business can get you through the door and close you.

A simple tip to get better at marketing is to track how many people come through the door.

This can be done by analysis, for example, if you have a landing page you can track on Google Analytics which one has a better click-through rate.

And, for sales the word is practice, practice, practice the more you sharpen your skills at sales the better you will eventually become.

What you need to consider, is that your first impression is vital, since it's your first way of showing the world, you exist and what you do.

This is why you need to have a reliable system that can hook people's attention and make them have the perception you want them to have of you.

Here are a few keys that you need to have in your marketing.

- Identify a problem in the marketplace.
- Provide a solution.
- Answer the question in the customer's mind "What's in it for me?" And show a sense of urgency as to why the customer should act now.

I also want to give you some pointers to consider towards external and internal communication.

- Sales.
- Marketing.
- Customer service.
- Investor relations.
- Public Relations.
- Sharing wins and success with the entire team.
- Regular meetings with employees.
- Human resources.

Just remember that communication is a two-way event, as an entrepreneur you have to listen to what the prospect has to say and try to provide a solution.

Systems

A body has multiple systems digestive system, respiratory system, circulatory system, and so on, without systems the body would become crippled or even die.

This is why having a system like this business triangle will help shine some light on what you need, as I said in part 1 the systems may be on different levels but don't think that you can slack off on any of them.

This is when you get into the league of big business, since it's no longer up to you to handle everything, you're going to have to find people who you can trust to manage each system on your behalf.

Unfortunately, many small businesses fail, since the owner feels like they can still be everywhere at once, which leads to the owner being spread too thin until a problem arises, and he or she can't be there to handle it.

A good businessperson can manage multiple systems effectively without becoming part of the system, a true business system is like a car.

The car doesn't depend upon one specific person to drive it, anyone who knows how to drive can do so.

The same is true for a big business, but not necessarily for small businesses, in most cases, the person in the small business is the system.

Every business, whether large or small, needs to have systems in place to enable it to conduct its day-to-day activities.

Even a self-employed person has to wear different hats to conduct his or her business, in essence, the self-employed person is all systems in one.

The better the system, the less dependent you become on others.

A good example of this is McDonald's It's the same everywhere in the world, and it's run by youths.

This is possible because of the excellent systems in place. McDonald's depends on systems, not people.

It's a very convenient thing, that systems are in the middle of the business triangle, since, they are the middleman that keeps the business together, and, can extend it.

This is why most entrepreneurs stay small, because they want to control everything, but this will lead to you not growing past yourself.

This is something I'm sure you don't want, you probably came into this entrepreneur life so you could work on something that you love, you never said you wanted your business to be clingy and never let you live.

Systems allow an entrepreneur to manage the team, systems allow the team to manage itself, and, systems create a standard for excellence.

An entrepreneur does not, and should not, know everything about his or her company.

But they should understand the systems in place, and, be able to recognize when a process is broken.

When one gets to the level of McDonald's or other major brands, one will have to create systems to manage systems.

The owner of McDonald's does not go into every McDonald's to see if the systems are holding the team, and, the quality together.

He or she looks at reports, the creation of the reporting process is a system, the true purpose of the reports is to identify a breakdown, or, success in a system.

For example, if the profit and loss statement show labor costs higher than what the system has deemed acceptable, then the owners know there is a breakdown.

The manager is notified of the breakdown and is asked why the labor system has failed, and what is being done to fix it.

As one can see, systems allow for a business to grow, be warned; however, the systems themself need to be watched, challenged, and held to a standard.

If one only manages through systems and not people, then cracks will develop, systems are to make the entrepreneur's job easier, not to make the entrepreneur lazy.

Entrepreneurs need a process to keep reevaluating their systems and to keep the human element present in the business, this is where the earlier chapter about team, mission, and leadership becomes important.

Type this link into your browser to get instant access to your answer to becoming an unstoppable business owner.

↓

bit.ly/bonusbook9

The Fastest Way On How To Make Your Business Sustainable And Profitable Part 4

And we are back with part 4 on how you can become a sustainable and profitable company, I've had fun making this for you :)

If you are going to put these tips, tricks, and techniques into action, please let me know how your business has improved.

Also, make sure to tell others about this book, so we can all gain great insights into becoming better CEOs.

As a quick refresher, this is what the business triangle looks like, now let's get started.

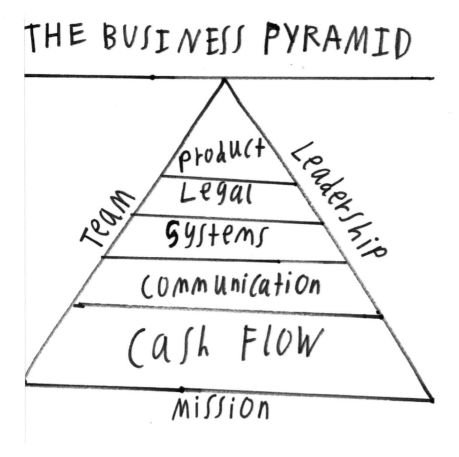

THE BUSINESS PYRAMID

Product
Legal
Systems
Communication
Cash Flow
Mission
Team
Leadership

Legal

This part of the triangle is the most painful since most people find out the hard way.

For example, if you put your blood, sweat, and tears into a product, but didn't secure the legal rights to it.

You could easily have it stolen from a competitor, and there's nothing you can do about it, or maybe a tenant slips on a coconut (Seriously this has happened).

And sues you, but you lack the legal structure to separate your personal belongings from the company, which leads to your car being taken.

A lot of people don't want to pay the high prices and maintenance of a legal team, but this is why, as I said earlier you want to have enough money to stay afloat.

Because the high-ticket purchases are extremely worth it, so please don't be one of those entrepreneurs that are penny wise but dollar foolish, your business will not appreciate it.

You probably have your logo and name trademarked, this is a good step since you know no one can copy or fake your name.

But the world of business is filled with intellectual bandits and people who steal your ideas.

It's said that Bill Gates became the richest man in the world with only an idea, in other words, he did not get rich by investing in real estate or factories.

He simply took the information, protected the information, and became the richest man in the world while still in his thirties.

The irony of it all is that he didn't even create the Microsoft operating system, he bought it from other programmers, sold it to IBM, and the rest is history.

Aristotle Onassis became a shipping giant with a simple legal document.

It was a contract from a large manufacturing company guaranteeing him the exclusive rights to transport its cargo all over the world, all he had was this document, he didn't own any ships.

Yet, with this legal document, he was able to convince the banks to lend him the money to buy the ships.

Where did he get the ships? He got them from the U.S. government after World War II.

The U.S. government had a surplus of Liberty and Victory class ships used to haul war materials from America to Europe, there was one catch, to buy the ships, the person needed to be a U.S. citizen, and Onassis was a Greek citizen.

Did that stop him? Of course, it didn't, by understanding the laws of big businesses, Onassis purchased the ships using a U.S. corporation he controlled.

This is another example of the laws being different depending on what stage you are in your organization.

I know you may be thinking "But Adventago I'm still small who would care?" I'm not saying you need to call in the supreme court.

But some type of protection will go a long way for you, and if you have it in place now, you can have peace of mind knowing it's already in position as the saying goes.

"Action Is Faster Than Reaction"

I also warn you, make sure to go to a trusted legal team, not your uncle who claims he knows a thing or two because he watched the Netflix series Suits.

If you don't, you could end up with legal problems in the future, which are a huge headache to redo, or even worse, give you no protection in court.

You also want to stay in contact with your legal team for any changes you will be making to your business.

This makes sure that all your legal documents are up to date, and all your latest assets are protected.

This is when franchising and network marketing can come in handy, and, help jump start your business, normally when you purchase a franchise, or, join a network marketing organization.

Most of the necessary legal documents to start and grow your business will be provided for you, this is a huge lifesaver on your time and money.

Because it allows you to focus your energy on developing your business, however, it's still a good idea to have a legal professional look over the documents.

I WANT YOUR MONEY

Another thing you want to think about is the tax structure for your company, since different structures pay differently in tax, this is a very important step for an entrepreneur.

Since if you make a wrong move, you'll be paying more than what you need to in taxes, which is a huge disadvantage, since you could be reinvesting that money to make your business better.

Here are some things you should think about when it comes to the tax structure of your business.

- Look at the good and bad of organizing your business as an LLC, LLP, C-CORP, and S-CORP.
- One is not better than another, they each have their strengths when it comes to what you do.
- You need to take action and make a decision, or you will automatically be given a sole proprietorship or general partnership.
- Make sure to consult a tax professional before deciding.

I know this last one may seem a bit silly, but you can't call your business Google.

This is why you need to do some research on your business name to see if it's available, then get it trademarked so no one can steal it.

Product

As you can see the product is the smallest, however, it's still important to your business.

There are a lot of great products that don't survive, which leads to the entrepreneur saying.

"This is better than the other company".

"No one has ever done this before".

"I have spent ages, making this!".

Robert Kiyosaki made a good example of this, when he would compare a McDonald's hamburger, he would say "Can you make a hamburger better than McDonald's"?

Most people would say yes, but Robert Kiyosaki would then ask, "Can you personally build a better business system than McDonald's?".

This is a test to show if the person is fixated on the product or a stable business system, the story behind this, is that there are many people out there who have far superior products.

But, only a few have created a system that allows them to push their product out there and make it sell like crazy.

Obviously, the product is important, or you would have nothing to sell, but things get difficult when the product gets all the entrepreneur's time and energy.

Your focus should be on the system and your team, together, this will make the product.

An easy way to know if your product would work is to find a problem in the world, once you have found that problem see if there is already a solution.

Then see how you can make the product better, as you can see you don't have to reinvent the wheel, simply find what works and try and make it better.

In Conclusion

Nooooo! We're finished, I know, unfortunately, all things must come to an end, but, now you have all the resources to be successful!

I hope you've gotten some great insights on what you can do to improve your business, but I have to be blunt with you.

Take Action

If you don't apply these tips, tricks, and, techniques, then I've just wasted my time, so please make sure that you put this advice into play and thank me later.

It would mean a lot to me if you shared this book with others, so we can spread the word and help each other.

I know this book gave you lots of insight on what to do next, but I understand that some of you want proven steps to achieving your success.

If you want to become a mighty business, you have the potential of being, and, having a consistent stream of income.

Type this link into your browser to go straight to a short video called.

↓

bit.ly/bonusbook9

<u>The profit boot camp,</u> this is where you can discover easy to implement secrets, on how you can increase your business's recognition, and, become a successful business owner.

What would becoming abundant in wealth, health, and happiness, do for you and others in your life? Let's make that a reality today!

Type this link into your browser to get instant access to your answer to becoming an unstoppable business owner.

↓

bit.ly/bonusbook9

Thank you for allowing me to serve you through these pages, it's truly been an honor, and I can't wait to see what you do with the frameworks that you've learned.

Come hit me up on social media, say hi, and please share with me how these tips, tricks, and techniques have changed your life.

Thanks,

Adventago

About The Author

Adventago (Real Name Elliott Goldson) started his first online business at the age of 16, while he was in college, within 2 months of starting, he had made his first $100 in a day online.

The funny thing about this story is that he wasn't even awake to see it, he had made this money completely in his sleep!

Over the past few months, he is trying to pursue not just one-time sales, but a constant stream of affiliate sales that would grant him the financial freedom that others can only dream of.

He has also gathered a small, but loyal following of a 1,000+ like-minded entrepreneurs and is the co-founder and CEO of a company called Adventago.

You can visit him online at Adventago.com

GET INSTANT ACCESS TO THE "SECRET" BONUS !!!

What's the secret?

✓ **Works for anyone, anytime, anywhere**

✓ **I will reveal my $460 a day blueprint to you!**

✓ **How to thrive even more during recession-times by knowing a simple 3-part concept**

✓ **What Every Elite Entrepreneur Does (whether they know it or not!)**

✓ **And many more tips, tricks, and techniques that YOU will love :)**

Type this link into your browser now to get instant access to the Adventago "SECRET" BONUS!!!

↓

bit.ly/bonusbook9

Have You Enjoyed The Secrets That You've <u>Learned</u> About In This Book?

If So, Then **Follow** Me On Social Media Where I Share My Inspirational Quotes And Best Entrepreneur Secrets At:

bit.ly/bonusbook9

Printed in Great Britain
by Amazon